DEPOSITION

Publication of this book was supported by a grant from the Greenwall Fund of The Academy of American Poets.

deposition

Katie Ford

Graywolf Press
SAINT PAUL, MINNESOTA

Publication of this volume is made possible in part by a grant provided by the Minnesota State Arts Board, through an appropriation by the Minnesota State Legislature, a grant from the Wells Fargo Foundation Minnesota, and a grant from the National Endowment for the Arts. Significant support has also been provided by the Bush Foundation; Marshall Field's Project Imagine with support from the Target Foundation; the McKnight Foundation; and other generous contributions from foundations, corporations, and individuals. To these organizations and individuals we offer our heartfelt thanks.

Special funding for this title has been provided by the Jerome Foundation and The Academy of American Poets.

Published by Graywolf Press
2402 University Avenue, Suite 203
Saint Paul, MN 55114

www.graywolfpress.org

Published in the United States of America

ISBN: 1-55597-374-4

2   4   6   8   9   7   5   3   1
First Graywolf Printing, 2002

Library of Congress Control Number: 2002102928

Cover design: Julie Metz

Cover art: Michelangelo, The Delphic Sibyl. Detail of the Sistine ceiling. Sistine Chapel,
          Vatican Palace, Vatican State
          Copyright Scala/Art Resource, NY

ACKNOWLEDGMENTS

Grateful acknowledgment is made to the editors of the following journals in which these poems first appeared:

Colorado Review: "Last Breath Underneath," "Last Breath on the Street," "Last Breath with Belief in It"

Denver Quarterly: "Last Breath Deciduous"

The Gamut (Harvard University): "Language of the Breaking Mind"

Northwest Review: "Last Breath and Diseases in the Wheat," "Last Breath at Dawn," "Last Breath I Tied a Cloth to a Tree"

Partisan Review: "On Taking the Body off the Cross"

Ploughshares: "Last Breath in Snowfall," "Last Breath with No Proof," "Last Breath on the Floor"

Post Road: "It's Late Here How Light Is Late Once You've Fallen," "Elegy to the Last Breath"

Salt Hill: "Nocturne"

Seneca Review: "That the Omissions Cast a Bluer Light"

Volt: "Last Breath Blue Nude"

"The Stations of the Cross" was commissioned by Harvard Divinity School in 2000.

For their generous teaching, I would like to thank Gordon D. Kaufman, John Desmond, Ben Mitchell, Tess Gallagher, Karen King, Sarah Coakley, and Peter Sacks. Sincere thanks also to Sarah Young Sentilles, Dudley Rose, Alex Schmidt, Ellen Haley, Susan Morgan, David Hall, and Jack and Christine Spong, all to whom I feel a great debt for their companionship and guidance. Thank you Katie Peterson and Suzanne Smith for your close readings of early drafts. Thank you, Jeffrey Shotts. Thanks and love above all to Mary Lynn, Michael and Brian Ford; also Kristin, David, Sam and Lily Martinson. And to Jorie Graham, my deepest gratitude.

FOR MY FAMILY

—————————————————————

FOR GORDON D. KAUFMAN

CONTENTS

III. The Wake

Deposition: (1) The action of putting down or deposing. (2) The taking down of the body of Christ from the cross; a representation of this in art. (3) The action of laying down, laying aside, or putting away (e.g. a burden). (4) The action of deposing or putting down from a position of dignity or authority; degradation, dethronement. (5) The giving of testimony upon oath in a court of law, or the testimony so given; *spec.* a statement in answer to interrogatories, constituting evidence, taken down in writing to be read in court as a substitute for the production of the witness. (6) The process of depositing or fact of being deposited by natural agency; precipitation, sediment.

All the dead voices.
They make a noise like wings.
Like leaves.
Like sand.
Like leaves.
Silence.
They all speak at once.
Each one to itself.
Silence.
Rather they whisper.
They rustle.
They murmur.
They rustle.
Silence.
What do they say?
They talk about their lives.
To have lived is not enough for them.
They have to talk about it.
To be dead is not enough for them.
It is not sufficient.

BECKETT

I

– THE FIRST GOSPEL –

PUT YOUR HANDS UPON YOUR EYES

Tell me how you know the truth, the master says.

I have become forgetful. I should not be trusted.

But tell me how you know.

I listen to something caught in the traplight.
It looks like a dry, fallen oak leaf. Then it is folding
in on itself, then back out,
one coarse moth-wing sloughing onto another.

But do you know the truth? the master asks.

I know what I'm seeing, I've seen it before —

something not quite dying, all night.
Also a hand leads to a body, which I cannot see —

And the truth of another? the master says.

— one hand among many, shoved through bars of a cattle car,
a loom of fingers and iron, decaying on the vertical
even as the cloth is made.

But how do you know the truth of another?

I wish what I think they would wish. I wish
God were not inside me.

I wish everything, I wish nothing were hidden from me of day.

And when there is no truth?

I have to hurry. I can't get the water cold enough.
Some of the burns are to the nerve. Whatever they have given her,
it isn't enough. I imagine her skin as a grid of land,
wheat and poppies and charred grass fill whichever square the wind
insists on. *You'll have to get my shoes,* she says. I get them, but I can't tell
where she is putting her weight, so I can't get them on.
She has no sensation in her feet.

How do you know when there is no truth?

There was no emergency in your voice, she says.
You talked to the doctor like there was no emergency,
and that's what I think this is.

LAST BREATH ON THE FLOOR

In the shower linoleum then floorboards then earth in which the depths
please send me away but see she cannot leave the house see what has been done

is thorough like something a cloth has been rinsed in or used for
tied across the eyes I have taken precautions leave no address leave no

trace water over the body entire but see yeast leavens the whole how could
this do harm this is the kingdom of God wet body sobbing on linoleum

sickness welling at any threshold what are you balking at she said
where would you be without us she said soon the killing felt like saving

a body burnt nerves burnt is this meaning is this to save
your life lose it I hear all night airplanes landing then go I heard but I am afraid

am panicked it is all of the time it is not some of the time do you know
what is used on the disobedient in some countries acid.

LAST BREATH WITH NO PROOF

What is unremembered may be lodged she said a child may not
recall but will act it out in play doll on the ground face against tile see how

he takes it by the hair the foot the tangled legs sweet mind made of tangled
legs and a patterned dress oh to have evidence to have the scent explained

birds trapped in the chimney rustle of wings and fire
or numbers etched into an arm show me where you were hurt I am asked

but I am simple unmarked remembering how
can one act out what happened in the mind how make

the mind alone in a house how show long silence what clock what song
is there for hollowness who hurt you

once the ticking the voices start she did he did my mind did
and the trespass begins again?

LARGENESS LIKE A HAND OVER A MOUTH

Heat rises out of the street-hollow, having passed through
the leaves in the grate patched and
pressed against the cell. They finger in and out of bars, jaundiced
with a pigment that cannot be processed.

Even what he didn't say he taught me, Matthew said.

Each pin of light sealed away, I can't see through to the ladder
attached to the wall beneath the street where floodlight
beams down the simple, cement corridor.

It feels like someone's hand is on my back, even when it is not on my back, he said.
*I would wake up . . . I wouldn't be asleep . . . I had no idea . . . felt the bed
beneath me and the floor. . . .*

The ice storm last night broke the reach of trees, I looked
out the window to see which way they broke, where
firs were, which direction sleet cracked down other deciduous spines,
which room would be safest if they fell. Then all night ice descending, encasing
each pine needle into a syringe. Smoke particles, fibers, silica, molds hovering
in the air pressed down again by frozen rain. Then I woke up and we
could leave our houses, a logging machine at dawn pulling
down branches dangling by some vein of inner wood. Soil indented
like hollow sockets where rain pushed down again, again,
collecting where the ground gave.

Have you ever seen someone who isn't there? Matthew asked.

I bend down to move the leaves away.

Someone else's words are in my mouth and I can't get them out, he said.

I hear so many things and see so many things I think I might be sick, he said.

I bend down to move the leaves away.

He sends me letters, he said.

They are frozen together. If I lift one they all begin to lift.

LAST BREATH IN SNOWFALL

I loved one person do you see the evergreen there in fog one by one
I was taught to withdraw first from him do you want to know how the mind

works under extreme cold ice forming on the eyelid or wind thrown
at me I felt every needle felt every breath I've seen a vision of you I was told

and disobedience in it in it nakedness you have not surrendered have not torn
his letters liken yourself therefore to the messenger who broke the tablets

take the letters and bring them but it is cold out our God is
a jealous God and so I did street warmed from beneath dark sky dark

hands took the photographs the letters twine-
bound tore them let them down through the grate what now I said just instruct

I have emptied am the earthen vessel no mementos no barrier make
straight the way of the Lord they said letters soaked with rainwater drifting

towards the city and twine a new twine binding me binding.

LAST BREATH WITH LIGHT ON THE LEAF

Beneath you could say battered leaf you might utter winter begins
when the veins show the skin can be seen through oh but it hurt my body

to think in their manner sacred thinning down of blood until gaps
in the wet string behold a sentence but I cannot read cannot make out
   whisk bowl sleep who is doing what

to whom if steam revolves eastward then go if westward stay tight fact
tight day steam around an invisible spine let the tea pour into the small

cup carry the dead or carry those who seem so I am so tired a mind a sheet
hung out in the wind is someone ill sleeping in the next room is it me

my body preparing the way steam widens is farther away pick up
the ceramic bowl set it down quietly with your palm memory coming back

do not take a drink if you do not know the field
the leaf is from no no take drink they said.

DARKEST WHERE IT IS EXPOSED TO THE MOST LIGHT

When I was an infant I barely cried and hardly moved, Matthew said.
A photograph bulged with darkroom water. I clamped onto it and pulled
the swollen sheet out of the basin, silver particles holding fast.

Red trees redder in the autumn minutes when dusk becomes dark.
Pines black or gone. To hold him was to hold a towel with hair and skindust
fixed between its thick threads. Water all down the bleached foreground,

the bleached background as pines shadowed into themselves
and the photograph began to dry its arch away. *So still I would fold into someone
else's body as if I were not a body of my own,* he said. *That's him, my father,* he said

as he pointed to the standing figure between the trees.
The trees pricked into the sky to let the insides out, Matthew clenched
his fists like bulbs in a cold earth. *And he put a warm hand on my face, don't*

misunderstand, my father said. . . . As we looked into the water I felt something
coming on in my body, a wind with a shudder behind it, an ocean with years
in it, as I felt that day on the wet street, the subway vibrating beneath,

leaves flattened on the cement like hands rolled over. *Only you can make yourself
feel something,* I was told, *no one can make you feel anything.* I didn't know
there would be a time I couldn't leave the house, I didn't know what words

could begin, the photograph as thick as skin from air to vein if skin could be
held up to the light, the latent image bruising into color. *I couldn't see him,*
Matthew said, *my body folded over the doorway.*

I hung the print on the line like a cloth pinned to a tree so I could find my way
back out from somewhere. Wire-line like an axis through the room
where things are caught and pulled towards a center —

The wall clock hummed, insects crawled out of walls.
I put the cover over the basin like a lid over an eye. *I began to realize every inch
of my skin he touched was one inch farther I would have to return from,* he said.

LAST BREATH ON THE STREET

On it rainwater and in it the moon I asked you to stay away first
sleep went then food then a huddle of crows on the concrete

steps up to my stoop please explain medically please I take my lamp
and keep watch therefore I prepared the oil I stand beneath a cluster

of years oh is there truth I have not waited for I am tired I want the lights
to go out so no one can find me blue plum buried in sand I cut off my hair
        I cut off my wick

prepare ye who is not the moon the truck that passes through digging
its wheels into the face caught in a concrete dune if you are not careful if

you do not let me alone your two eyes will surely
in the end be completely opened what then?

LAST BREATH WITH BELIEF IN IT

They blindfolded her put her in the closet for a month
they didn't want her dead grass pulled out they wanted her to believe

grass thickening a field once or twice dark month they had her
sit with them long wooden table why stray why desire and light came

through the torn robe over her eyes out of which birds were cut out of which
hoods she listened into the night long into the closet she even thought blessing

even thought grace towards her she began to trust they had faith had truth
years pass ocean and winds and moons pass she is cold she pulls she opens

her closet any morning sees the dark corner she could crawl into is it
over now but I beseech thee help her stop believing

help me sometimes I want back in.

LAST BREATH BLUE NUDE

As if the line of your body means you are not made of torn things onlookers
can consume what is pieced unpieced in you dear turning away dear story

unmade in her she is unmaking something with the exactitude of a black line
she is whispering into her knees retreats into the oblonged grid of skin

where it is mapped out truth has become the weight of a body unappeasable
facts undraw her she cannot listen to what has unfolded in stages layer by layer

of wet wing shredded down onto canvas in an unjustifiable shade of clouds
and sky why is it she is in this position of having to salvage what is left of herself

there where the forehead is fused to the knee she is made of one unrevelatory
  border
like the line the crow makes in something dead to open its thick trunk

the internal rising out so literal so
she turns away this is how she has been made ravenous maker he has gutted her

and oh she cannot look her bruised grafts of skin she knows
  no hand can touch her
would go right through as if she were made of more water than sand maker
  what lodgment

is this that she cannot turn to you maker she cannot move you have made
her this way so you will never have to face her

shattered iris diminished pupil against the knees how dark it is.

SOMEONE HAS TO TELL HER
THERE IS NO ANSWERING BACK

I took the ink and made a print of the only body
I knew how to make: a silhouette, a body wrapped
in a blanket, in fog, behind a shade
pulled past the bottom edge of the window. Undone
like a scroll with its rod bare, as her shade was
in the building across the street.
My kitchen faced her, and the slanted light
at dawn passed straight into my sink.
The woman looked up into the ceiling
as if there were one unbending bone
from her pelvis to her chin.
The red trees around her window
dim and muted like the underside of a tongue. Matthew
said he watched his father do the dishes
as if nothing had happened — *Come here, you've misunderstood,*
what happened is not what you think —
as he turned from the sink and saw his son
with his back pressed against the wall.
Matthew said he would hold whatever position his father left him in.
Each faceless dish in his father's hands, drying, drying.
Then his hands, the palm first, each finger,
the in-between, the beneath of the nail
where cells separate and multiply. *I'm trying to save you from a life.*
I thought she would cry out, drop her jaw
and relieve the bone. I waited to hear something breakable
break. Glass birds off her shelf, the hourglass lamp
divided on the linoleum. Or a hinge might give,
and the door would fall off its own device, the coil rolling,
the spring finding its own equilibrium.

16

No one told me, *use this ink, make a body.* And now my hands
in the sink, trying to wash it off the page, birds in the light
like rags torn from black cloth,
descending onto the nest of the eye. But in water ink spreads
its thin body to fill each notch of page
with a swollen darkness, because she did not open her mouth,
she was as still as the last shred of cloth
the birds were torn from. No cry — for what,
my God, would a cry do?

LAST BREATH AND DISEASES IN THE WHEAT

As fire starts is soundless up the curtain as whispering down the hall
going to see what about what now what more can this house hold this is how

the rust the soot began on the grain at dusk a silhouette at dawn
too bright to see what the glumes the hard grain have on them besides morning

red spring wheat darkening like limbs caught in a door one end pale
one pulsing more blood too much for any vein early leaves early height

you have made me quiet have made me careful carefully
the rabbi said it is not for you to return to the God abusive listen ash in sky

settles on the wheat listen for what is doing what to whom.

LAST BREATH UNDERNEATH

It occurs to me you can hear me even here under water where I
cannot slip the timbre voice of past I am weary enough when I come up

I may not open my eyes open my one argument my unmythic
complaint *what else does the world want but to pass through us* but I am
    worn out world through

flesh yeast through a sieve residue of a past season
brown leaves cone themselves into wrists January now too late to drop

ice fixes the hold kyrie eleison fixes the hold chimneys hold sky
envelope holds a message I hold my breath I was baptized at infancy

they said you must go under again their argument a cage strapped
to a tree for a woman to crawl into be dunked in

just enough for thankfulness to braid into
each atom constructed crisis constructed saving into tissue into lung.

LAST BREATH WANTS THE MATERIAL

If mental properties were physical properties I'd hand you the
poisonous bird last on earth chipping away at skin metabolic activities churn

behold a colony in the tissue be still and know the toxin builds
a nation in me though difficult to isolate though difficult to inhabit

please be nomadic come to me although I understand that through
the horses the cattle the antitoxin is harvested through these I am touched

medically I am told swallow this and that white film white photo
warming to show where the harm is but your skin is so smooth they say
       but we cannot find

anything they say light heat age affects the toxin it shifts it shifts
it can look like bone like a muscle flushed with blood I hold my stomach

it's your mind that's the problem it triggers the toxin they say
if mental properties were physical properties I would hold my mind

the bird let it peck until through.

LAST BREATH AT DAWN

I don't know what has been absolved what not I hear people still with
no beating thing called a heart feel a warm hand on my back evil comfort
        comfort

thy people I need someone to believe me I dig the iron
into the neck of the shirt beneath the collar against the windpipe red birds

pecking their faces into cracks outside torch-shaped trees losing
their minds dry roots pull out is anywhere wet I have not slept at all no one

will wake in the house for hours earth against deeper earth
molten story a river I don't know where you are maybe you wake up next

to your life water in its pod coins on the aspen turning
all things straightened all things —

DO YOU LOOK OUT THE WINDOW
BECAUSE YOU FEEL WATCHED?

You think summer fires will take all the wheat.
Listen to me: What you are looking for cannot be
found now. It's winter, look at the snow —

      But feel the snow.
      It's dry as dust.

This is how it is with the anxious. What will not happen is
happening all of the time. The glare
off the snow mid-morning a warped station of white,

a land that cannot be mapped because to look at it
changes the eye. If you knew anything about fire
you would know winter hardly matters.

      And if you knew winter
      you would know it
      cannot be undone, only
      pressed beneath the fields.

II

– THE STATIONS OF THE CROSS –

gli occhi miei stanchi di mirar, non sazi
(for my eyes are tired from looking, but not full)

P E T R A R C H

Station the First: He is condemned to death

PETITION

I walked the horse around the hayfield even though it had yellow eyes
and would hardly let me touch it. I brushed the field dust off,
soon it was there again. If I kept watch, watch would be kept over me,
I thought. Plums rotted the branch, every few minutes I passed them.
I didn't want anyone to come near me while I was in those fields.

Station the Second: He takes up his cross

THAT THE OMISSIONS CAST A BLUER LIGHT

There would have been birds there.
       Ask the text
where have they gone?

Not a setting but a loom made loose where someone has touched it, then left.
       Ask the loom
what is it like to have things made over you?

Belief and doubt on the form of faces.
       Ask the faces
which is which?

A woman walked away while the others wailed.
       Ask her
what do you know he cannot give you?

The morning came as cloudless irony.
       Ask the sun over the hill
do you find yourself irrelevant?

Then meanings: one dome over the next until there was dusk.
       Ask the ashen sky
how is it to be always and never touched?

Station the Third: He falls the first time

HOW IT IS TO BE IN THE BODY

Look there, she says, but by the time you look
there are no birds. No blue clones, givens
undoing the ground.
Only this winged vanishing
locating the dying thing
in the wheat. The fire in the field rolls out
its bloody gown until each grainskin pulls
off shaft. The outside of desire is
her saying, *be applicable, cloud.* (There are verbs
but they are not willing.)

— —

Hot light. Presumed negligence — belief studded with cysts of ash.
(No not belief just the scrolls are damaged or yes belief too.)

— —

Pressed now into the land like wax and hair flattened by a clay signet.

— —

The inside of desire: but the empty coat
is too small. Putting it back in the trunk fold by fold putting
it back. Nothing
applicable. Just the body with its cause
and effect, smoothed down like one wool arm tucked
under the next. One hand sinking into the trunk then
the next. One question then the next then
the landscape
cleansed but not yielding.

— —

Then two voices murmured out of dark throats, each
distended like a conceptual temple:

Hers
        Are you?
Yours
        I'm —

Station the Fourth: He meets his afflicted mother

THE BRACE

It was that day in the graveyard when there was no hole and we had to leave the casket above ground. There was a cloud like a rip in the sky and stone that had nothing to mark. The grass was not cut away, the rock was not set in place like a patch or cemented window. It could not begin to sink into the ground with growth below starting to push up until it had nowhere to go. Our eyes on the box as if a structure had never held her in before. But I remember, I was there. Standing in the closet with the door cracked, my hand over my mouth to muffle the breathing. I saw, there, on the chair. The brace that would hold her spine together, its white halves like shutters latched on a house where the things that are spoken cannot change anything. She loomed it together herself first with the hooks on the front. Then twisted it around to the back, the last bit done up by feel. This is how it is done.

Station the Fifth: The cross is laid on Simon of Cyrene

THE HISTORICAL METHOD

1
The sun down. The maple relit
by the streetlamp.

1a
A photograph of a bonfire.

2
Someone's put a cement block on the edge but
partly in the pond. A girl
sits on it. The water seems

3
to rise and sink
like the shoulder of something sleeping,

3a
even though that can't be.

4
The pond is empty or slow fish swim under the double-faced screen of water.

5
So that autumn is literal I pick up what I want
from the fallen things.

6
Everything feels watched by the black sky reordering us.

7

The glass light hums in the glass case.

7a

Light torsos the maple

7b

for those who name the outline and not
the interior of the body.

8

The pure noun. The am-

9

phibian in the pond, out of the pond, one name
for two places,

10

brushes the edges like the tangential God, because it wasn't assigned
the second-day waters nor the third-day earth
when the structure had been built but there was nothing
to fill it.

11

The girl rubs her hands together,
sticks for fire

11a

that disappears after it has consumed its body.

12
(The light on the leaf.)

13
Disappears

14
the instant it's through, vanishes

15
like the cross after it was done having a body on it and went unrecorded

16
thereafter.

Station the Sixth: A woman wipes his face

A WOMAN WIPES THE FACE OF JESUS

This comes out of folklore.
Invented because tenderness at times
must be written in. There was a woman.
There was a cross. But in fact
they have hung him too high
to be touched.

Station the Seventh: He falls a second time

LANGUAGE OF THE BREAKING MIND

strapped down she cannot stop screaming
two red jays weigh down a limb outside the window

the ones who work here know what to do I do not
know what to do

they say *what she sees is real to her what she sees is scaring her*
I nod yes and listen to her talk about the oceans in the walls and *where is Matthew*

the birds go the limb buoys back up like the oar that came to the surface
when we were collecting stones in the cove and thought things could be kept

if only she had answered their questions if only she had not run
down the hallway brought back arched like a jib with wind behind

wrists cuffed to a wheelchair her eyes sunken back then shot open
like yours when the man who followed you was standing in your doorway

she is sure of something needs to tell us something like an urgent parcel
of clothes sent to the mother of a missing child brown paper ravaged but

the tape will not break without a knife into it once through she unravels
the paper with a sudden slowness as if ashes or glass birds were inside

unfolding unfolding until a red wool sweater is uncovered and she has to
say *no this does not belong to her* —

Station the Eighth: He meets the women of Jerusalem

LAMENTATION

If you see anything see dusk pass
Over water and stones. Oak leaves
More blue than green hang from a tree.

I can't cry for someone I don't know.
Even the woman from the borough who threw herself
Into this wide river, even the child inside her.

But when I walk along this bank
During a summer drought, the dry stones
Look like faces.

Station the Ninth: He falls for the third time

NOCTURNE

I can see the whole city, lights edging the harbor like yellow pins in uneven
cloth beneath the hands of a woman cutting the measured lines of a dress;
when it is done she will put it on to see if it fits.

Blackish harbor, facing east no facing west, lights
meaning anything but *exit,* ships waiting for dawn so they can navigate out,
fog in the cove, cigarette smoke in this

restaurant at the top of the Prudential.
Please do not use your hands to touch my face.
Please let me be decided.

Lights fringe the harbor, she is sewing a dress a centimeter too small,
you tap off ashes, I lean into the winding smoke because it is not myth,
because I can bring even an ending into the body.

The city now unsettled beneath us. My face eye-level in the glass.

Please help me get up from this table.
Please put that thing down.

She turns an edge under. Smoke is taken in, smoke like a text
etched into two tablets of lung. Here, and here: Sinai.

Atoms fill their due portion of each ash.

Please look somewhere else with your eyes.

She undoes the knotted threads where she wants the blue and gray strips closer to each other, crop of lavender, dust.

Please do not touch my face.

When she is done she takes off her clothes, raises her arms to get into the dress,

Please do not touch my face.

The harbor at its darkest, stillest, like a question in a throat.

Station the Tenth: He is stripped of his garments

ON BEING DEVOUT

Fire in its swarm took everything.
Through my kitchen window I watched,
no better view. Paint, roof, ceiling taken. Smoke
answering. The chimney upright in the char
of things. No use guessing what has done this. Sealant
giving out an undressing of
the body's nearly former self. Light replacing
form, narrative muttered where the corners were.

Thick cypress dripping and dripping.

A bare maple blooms with smoke.

(Will have to look, find cause.)

Wind catching, catching.

But I am already tired of looking: the fire, the house, the sky not having to.

I have to. I have found debris

being made. Look inside the piles. White sky
emptied of a house. More sky
now, more coming. Shouting
on the street. Debris about.
Trees unblocked. Loosened
frame. Light snow into
the gutted body, so obedient, coming
despite.

Station the Eleventh: He is nailed to the cross

FLESH

One breath began the world, one can take it back again.

(Ask if I remember when.)

I would have preferred the void. At least there you know there is nothing to find.

Now the sun lowers behind the river, bare
sycamores fill with sundown. Long bones
like iron branching in the stained glass
of the incarnation. There is only so long I can watch
things go down.

(Also ask what happened to my body.)

Some leaves only show after the sun is fully down, the light violet
and blue, a second river, one with no drawbridge to lean over and look.
The brown geese walk on the frozen river, shuddering to dry
their simple bodies.

(Also about my body.)

In the winter the last leaves fall, or remain
clipped to the branch, lobes opening
from the base of each swollen leafstalk. No seed
this time of year, tight and inscripted within,
to tell it what it is.

(Ask me what I believe.)

(What was said about disobedience.)

When I speak I hear a rustling of leaves, of wings and ashes, of someone straightening something undone. A sweeping up of the left ungathered, and the bridge is lifted by its inner chains.

If you are speaking I cannot hear you.

Station the Twelfth: He dies on the cross

THE HANDS OF THE BODY WITHOUT THE BODY,
AND NOTHING TO HOLD

How she worked was this: *Give me what I need, I am bending down,*
this is the last thing I'll ask — a fossilized backbone, a clay vase, a cylinder of darker

ground where oil seeped out of a jar. Something — the hollow of her lung? —
with whispering inside it, *bring me something, bring me something.* An ax in her

hand digging into the hillside, poison oak everywhere. Her body everywhere
covered with rash. In her sack of air the whispering warped and tripled

by a thin border: *This is the site. This is the thing. Let, to those who have, more be given.*
It's that she wants something solved, ended, even darkly, a crow stopped by glass.

The gash tearing further, tissue exposed. Rocks grind under
the wheel of a truck coming uphill. Even an umbilical cord of exhaust

cannot pull her into the unsought present.
Polluted metaphysic, bolt where the engine gives out.

Night begins, untrustworthy for what it does to the eye, the pupil blown open,
the iris branching its genealogy. Dust climbs,

her skin the color of the hill, hives beneath, red poppies in smog.
She thinks, *the rip in the fabric would prove—the linen preserved would show—*
    the buried

text would give — (and so on). Blackbirds huddle beneath the parked truck (*Bring me*
something.), each wing a jag of obsidian sheeting off its rock (*Anything.*).

The broken-up hill bears its spine, its dream of ladders —
(The self wants to find the self elsewhere.). She bears down on its rounded bone.

Why do you seek the living among the dead? She bears down. *What do you seek?*
She bears down. *Why are you afraid?*

My hand is torn open, I have nothing to show. *Why are you afraid?* I am
afraid I might find the entire stone church beneath this hill. Altar, crypt, bodies

curled like leaves in ash. I am scared I will find it all and still it will not move me.

Station the Thirteenth: The body is placed in the arms of his mother

ON TAKING THE BODY OFF THE CROSS

The moon seems close, the docks are saturated,
a small boat rocking like a light seed caught
by the torn thread of a web, its catching
noticed only as what has not been heard,
like delay, rain on snow, the hiding
of an envelope beneath ground. There are
night-moths over the water. Their shadow
of pieces hovers in the instinct
of what mass might be. Loose logs thud
up in the dock — wet wood on wet wood,
like a falling horse, its thin legs tangled,
its belly a brown sack that hits ground
first, the freight of a sandbag we lift
and throw so we can go on living here.

Station the Fourteenth: He is laid in the tomb

DOCTRINE

     (Air neither in nor out where the bodies are.)

Live pine branches carried from the street to the pile of debris.

     (A bird caught in fresh cement.)

The sea is blue.

Winter as a line of ink.

A cave in the side of the canyon. The view from there —
others are dropping *consider how awful*.

She is told *do not look away*, yet she ticks with doubt.

     (Another branch.)

The sea is a stone blue sheet of hooks.

Put the body into the crypt quickly. Shut the iron door. Latch the iron bar.

A woman wants something but —

     (The bird sinking.)

Not admitting pain.

Longing suspended like a pendulum behind glass.

(Dusk fills the canyon but not the cave.)

The sea is platinum where the flock makes an arrow of shadows.

Not admitting pleasure.

     (Pain lasting, the pleasure —)

The sea is bluish.

     (And the ocean.)

Spring divided from summer divided from autumn divided from winter
                               divided from spring.

The bird petrified.

     (No more branches.)

Air neither in nor out.

III

– THE WAKE –

What shall I take to witness for thee?
What shall I liken to thee?

LAMENTATIONS

THE SHROUD OF TURIN

You see I am not certain you see the cloth held up to the light betrays
an imprint of the whole body glands seeping out what was in

them before death consider where else would it go but out I suppose this
is what I will do when I miss the beloved lay his bedsheet on carpet take

my hands brace my body over it see my shadow twine into his
a hawk spans the undiminished canyon darkens all of it from above

this bolt of linen undone as time fades into as it was in the beginning
hawk at birth unstreaked come methodology of absence how something grows

more absent what will fill what will be avian be predatory I am not certain what
to do here above the knitted sheet knitted tight enough to hold the shade

passing through to the upper limit of descent there has been scientific inquiry
into the ancient bedclothes it can't be they say but then the realism of the print

when photographed one replies someone was here I would cross open spaces
for fictitious evidence yes he was here not Jesus no it's not him that I want

I confess it is not his cloth I pass my body over oh I sense the spread of a hand
here bird-shadow here there will be miles and miles between us between

Golgotha and Italy hills and dusks and waters see they insist we know
what a shroud is what likeness is please do not prove anything away

please someone was here the body is gone it may not come back
the woman in front of the glass around the shroud see how she wants to take

it in her hands wants to know the loom it was made on
how when I am in your hands you know.

LAST BREATH DECIDUOUS

For instance he sees his uncle shot for instance 55 years
ago and rituals behind him marriage behind a fresh mound outside

and a small dried plot next there were children behind him baptisms
he was pushed by his aunt get beneath the bed he looks from there through

bedlace yellowed on the edge like sweated hoods I can't even hear
a southern accent today he says and this is 50 years this is historic

add to that blindness add to that north add to that prayer
to that guilt be still bedlace be still floorboard add to that dust kicked

up as he slid beneath the frame and not wanting to see but not
able to look away for instance red is farther along than orange orange is farther

than yellow yellow than green we watch along the stations
why must we watch with the tidy eye breath in and out face flushed

then emptied but where the eye stores its things nothing is emptied.

WHEN THE TREES ARE GONE

Fire in the trees splits them
open like body bags. They heap
into piles, tips pointing to the blue mountains bruising
the edge of the valley, pointing to the river just
before it runs into the walled arc of the dam, to where I know
water that far off is useless.

1. What does its task to the trees is true.
2. What pulses so you can make out a body is true.

Fire in the trees splits them open,
the pine-splints clean and stripped downwards
like a photograph of something caught
falling. Is it fire, is it wood
that makes the sound of the mussel I cracked off a rock yesterday?
Only a half-body away, my hand on the rock, wrenching
an armor of white off the stone haystack.

3. A crack and then again a crack of heat, of pine, of a bag opened, of the shell.
4. What makes a sound is true.
5. In me the sound of something repeatedly done to another thing.

Fire in the trees splits them.
I took the shells from the rock, quickly as if the tide
were coming in. My arms were full because of what I did.

6. The tide was out. The tide was out.
7. The sky becomes larger, more true, becomes the shape of the body
   it lost, hollows everywhere.

What will I have to say to the man who tells me,
when we watch the ashes cool acre by acre, the fire
having consumed each arrow-pine standing and fallen,

It was like this the evening my wife died. She filled the whole bed.
I would turn to her, then remember she
was wrapped in a blanket in the front hall. There was no
arch in her spine. The blanket had smoothed over each edge
and curve of her face like a leaf enclosing its knotted buds.
I turned to her again and again until morning, when they came to take
her away. Just wait. Tomorrow
when you wake up, you will see the trees
where they used to be.

THE MANNER IN WHICH ONE IS ABLE TO SEE

The forest has burned down. There are
birds, dangling, as people
begin to come out of their houses on the ridge
to look and to count.

Stems from fallen trees snag into
the river where a long wrist of soot splits around a rock.

(Inside the stems, inside the coal
cells drift like eyes wandering
the parameter of each wall.)

Tell me what it is to dangle, the master says.

Birds try to return to something gone.

LAST BREATH DEPOSITION

Please I am forthright last night he slept on a quilt beside my bed in this way
he meant for me not to be alone in this way I was moreso before tonight

we climbed down to the eastern shore below the quarry where all that could be
taken had been now just a dome of missing earth there were rocks

in front of us but more under water no sand pulsing with its intake
of water and its pull back into the sharp hooks of sea I knew then there

was knowledge in me then the January air so sharpened I looked into
the sky to see what might have been written there nothing but insects far off

their bodies deposing what must be brought low before our eyes
he lifted a small rock from the stack to throw its simple body into the water

to throw the decomposition of what came
from on high far away from us.

LAST BREATH I CHOSE FIRE

Turn your entire head think bone around eye think hardening skin
stiffening facial disk the bridge is gone cables cut flung rippling the pull gone

a snake undoing from its tree if they say the body will be raised burn
the body if no clothing sticks if no sticks hair if no hair lashes on the eye

the pond is so very still no wind no pollen inside the wind fish curl
in a nest of weeds sun curls further blackbirds will take the husk my husk

I imagine what is left of me patched into a robe stitched a second skin
for the pale self here just minutes ago she is on the page she is off

and the monk will put it on will mourn will make a day of it
see we have been expecting her but I abandoned the hive the heap of sticks

and what fathered it I left even the idea of father
at the monastery when I wanted to leave all the doors opened to locked

from the outside gardens.

LAST BREATH WITH A HILLSIDE

Tell me again how a pressure is exerted how cells divide
how a body is not its own in the absence of safety the gunman in the troop

strokes the clear face of the dime anything risen embossed in metal
he believes he believes skin over an edge the forehead lip chin get him back

to his platoon quickly after the leg the gangrene cools darkens
and he can drag it behind him just get him back to the group it is best

there he will feel into a breast pocket find a dime believe omens
signs in absence of security see the cloud how it parts see the moon how it

was not there you have to believe me and now is there just as the bullet
buried itself into the hillside cells die in the leg by the second mass death

tissues bloodless this is not a simple wound this is dirt and wound
dirt from the hillside green hillside grass bending that took the bullet into

the mind.

IT'S LATE HERE HOW LIGHT IS LATE ONCE YOU'VE FALLEN

I began to see a gauze over the wheat.
The fields were darker where an owl had flown
against the window of the house. I bent
and put my fingers into its cold down. Hundreds
of tiny spiders unhinged their bodies, bodies
which are their minds, as my body was,
moving like a city wanting to go inside
all the cavities. Moths too,
some were caught and tried to flutter out. I put my hands in
farther. Felt the body of the thing, the owl. At first it seemed
so dead. Then, not at all — either my fingers
pulsing with blood or its breathing. I held
breath too, like a mother bent to the crib. Nothing.
Then maybe something. I looked behind me,
my fingers making out bones, twigs of what was left, glazed
by faint morning stars that pocked the sky when I looked up, stars
in their arc of recovery from being seen
into being hidden again by light. Some of its feathers
were matted. When it had hit the window
the storm layers shook the space between. *Lie still,* I said to you,
I'll go see. But all I really wanted
was to leave that house, your
steady rise and fall of breathing inside it.
Outside, there was no farther in to go. It must have been
a barn owl with its heartish face
and lightly speckled underneath, its feathers
thin leaves spotted with mold. I pulled out my hands
and spread its wings out full, the soft body
exposed. And that's when I was sure it was dead —
when it let me do that to its body.

LAST BREATH I TIED A CLOTH TO A TREE

to find my way out after storms after thaws I remember before
when I could look out the window see haze in the hills grass

burnt with frost think winter and night that is all it stood for
nothing else a bird dangling in the open sky was not me the valley curved

by sun by hard weather bad water was not me someone
speak my name the acres grow deafness

the stag alone stares into the sounds that are left let me touch
someone's skin I stepped over the heat from the grate

dark patch on cement dark indentation and slats
your iron loom is giving out soot will gather rain will push red trees will

grow redder the loom gives where have you been
the Lord will say where have you been I will answer.

LAST BREATH UNDONE FOR ANOTHER

Soot gathers in the grate the child she carries
is cold is unshapely its dress falls into her face

no one told me I could be veiled no one asked
can I touch the skin you hide and no one did whereby

the argument stood we did nothing to you but see
the mother demands of Elisha didn't I say don't mislead

me see now the child you promised is dead the prophet puts his mouth
on the child's mouth his eyes on her eyes his hands on her hands and

the body warms back red clay in the sun but what about black soil
beneath the reaches?

O EVERYTHING GOES BLACK

A pattern on the back of my eyelid coils like a fingerprint, I made
a mistake, it is not my own. The blood up between my eyes, I can't see,
I sit between people, between pillars of the cathedral between
which the immaculate spreads her blue wing-sleeves into as much sky
as there is. Small blue lights edge the church and the eyeless Christ hangs,
his sockets darkening into shaded tombs. Darkness coiling,
my eyes coiling, a wind with sand in it scrolling up and down
a body, hiding that body until it could be anyone, and is.
Even whom I do not live with I live with now. Don't say I don't
speak to you: I speak to you.

LAST BREATH ICE AND WOODS

I don't know why the ice came no one knows
why the sky opened its gulf and then branches against windows

and trucks and buses down the hill so slowly for the ridge is at its end
inside put your body between the glass door and your child

 hush hush those are just sticks sleep sleep mind
I was told you see me I have no reason to say that is so

unless seeing is how the owl sees at dark
everything that moves in the grass is prey.

TAKE YOUR HANDS OFF YOUR EYES

What the rain is, I remember. A rain
with crows in it, beating
their wings against a sky that does nothing
to help them. Only instinct
helps them, only tiredness
teaches them what shape will cut the current
of air.

What did you see? the master asked.

I heard birds shriek like a drawbridge hoisted against the rain.
It was as if many bodies were trying to be one body,
as if asters in the field do not die separately.

What did you see? the master asked.

Then it was dusk, the rain stopped as the birds
disappeared from sight. I believed
two events so near each other must be related.
The moths came out; some were dim, brown.
Others had adapted the colors of poison,
red and yellow snaking into wing. The poison itself
no longer mattered, only its color.
Still, the moths could not stop
their wings from being reduced
in motion on the side hit by light. So I caught them.

Describe the light, the master said.

I believed the truth could not be
so terrible.

Describe the light.

I didn't believe anything I was told. I didn't want to be told anything.

The moths hit the glass walls of the jar and left a smudge
of pollen, having carried off what they never meant to take,
the print part moth, part something else.

Describe the light.

I was tired. I took everything
I had away from that kind of light.

Are you still hearing things? the master asked.

I am not forgetful.

Are you hearing things?

You should know by now who I am.

What do you hear?

The folds of their bodies creased
into the air like shreds of a text torn
and lifted away at dark. It was when I let them out
that I let the voices out.

ELEGY TO THE LAST BREATH

The heron in the marsh extends
its striped neck its dagger-bill points into the sky during its long sleep

it will be mistaken for a reed I had nothing
to hide by I had to move my body instead

into a space
that was not a space between the fallen-down wall and the grass

cement and grass pressed against my lungs collapsing
if owls fly among the ruins as it is written I had nothing to see them with

grass had no room to shudder corridors flattened
in the dirt like veins pinched off by weight

Lord of harvest and of land if you commanded this
rest now it has come to pass.

The definition of "deposition" comes from *The Oxford English Dictionary*.

The opening epigraph is from Samuel Beckett's *Waiting for Godot* (New York: Grove/Atlantic Inc., 1976).

"Put Your Hands upon Your Eyes" is a line from the *Apocalypse of Peter,* translated by James Brashler and Roger A. Bullard, *The Nag Hammadi Library*. James M. Robinson, ed. (San Francisco: HarperCollins, 1978).

"Last Breath with No Proof," "Last Breath with Belief in It," and "Last Breath with a Hillside" refer to narratives and psychological studies from Judith Herman's book, *Trauma and Recovery* (New York: Basic Books, 1992).

"Last Breath Blue Nude" is after Picasso, and indebted to Suzanne Smith.

"Last Breath and Diseases in the Wheat" includes the title of Linda Gregg's book, *Too Bright to See* (Saint Paul: Graywolf Press, 1981, 2002).

"Last Breath Underneath" quotes Rainer Maria Rilke.

"Last Breath at Dawn" adapts the line "comfort comfort/thy people" from Isaiah 40:1.

The epigraph for "The Stations of the Cross" is from Petrarch's 190th Sonnet. The titles of "The Stations of the Cross," with some revisions, follow the order of service as found in the *Episcopal Book of Occasional Services.* This set of poems was commissioned by Harvard Divinity School and displayed alongside the encaustic paintings of Sarah Young Sentilles in Andover Chapel, Harvard Divinity School.

The epigraph for "The Wake" is from Lamentations 2:13.

"Last Breath Deciduous" is for Tony Coleman.

"Last Breath Undone for Another" refers to II Kings 4:27, where the prophet Elisha resurrects a child.

"Elegy to the Last Breath" takes the lines "owls fly among the ruins" and "Lord of harvest and of land" from Psalms 102:6.

KATIE FORD grew up in Oregon and was educated at Whitman College and Harvard University, where she received a master of divinity degree. Her poems have been printed in *Ploughshares, Colorado Review,* and *Partisan Review,* among other journals. She currently studies poetry and teaches creative writing at the University of Iowa. *Deposition* is her first book.

The text has been set in Granjon, a typeface drawn by George William Jones and issued by Linotype in 1928. It is based on the work of Claude Garamond (c. 1490–1561), and Robert Granjon (c. 1513–1590), both French typecutters.

Book design by Wendy Holdman
Typesetting by Stanton Publication Services, Inc., St. Paul, Minnesota
Manufactured by Sheridan Books on acid-free paper

Graywolf Press is a not-for-profit, independent press. The books we publish include poetry, literary fiction, and cultural criticism. We are less interested in bestsellers than in talented writers who display a freshness of voice coupled with a distinct vision. We believe these are the very qualities essential to shape a vital and diverse culture.

Thankfully, many of our readers feel the same way. They have shown this through their desire to buy books by Graywolf writers; they have told us this themselves through their e-mail notes and at author events; and they have reinforced their commitment by contributing financial support, in small amounts and in large amounts, and joining the "Friends of Graywolf."

If you enjoyed this book and wish to learn more about Graywolf Press, we invite you to ask your bookseller or librarian about further Graywolf titles; or to contact us for a free catalog; or to visit our award-winning web site that features information about our forthcoming books.

We would also like to invite you to consider joining the hundreds of individuals who are already "Friends of Graywolf" by contributing to our membership program. Individual donations of any size are significant to us: they tell us that you believe that the kind of publishing we do *matters*. Our web site gives you many more details about the benefits you will enjoy as a "Friend of Graywolf"; but if you do not have online access, we urge you to contact us for a copy of our membership brochure.

www.graywolfpress.org

Graywolf Press
2402 University Avenue, Suite 203
Saint Paul, MN 55114
Phone: (651) 641-0077
Fax: (651) 641-0036
E-mail: wolves@graywolfpress.org

Graywolf Press is dedicated to the creation and promotion of thoughtful and imaginative contemporary literature essential to a vital and diverse culture. For further information, visit us online at: **www.graywolfpress.org**.

Other Graywolf titles you might enjoy:

As for Dream
by Saskia Hamilton

Too Bright to See & Alma
by Linda Gregg

Blind Huber
by Nick Flynn

Pastoral
by Carl Phillips

No Shelter: The Selected Poems of Pura López-Colomé,
translated by Forrest Gander